An Appleseed Editions book

First published in 2013 by Franklin Watts
338 Euston Road, London NW1 3BH

Franklin Watts Australia
Hachette Children's Books
Level 17/207 Kent St, Sydney, NSW 2000

© 2013 Appleseed Editions

Created by Appleseed Editions Ltd,
Well House, Friars Hill, Guestling,
East Sussex TN35 4ET

Designed and illustrated by Guy Callaby
Edited by Mary-Jane Wilkins

ISBN 978 14451 2176 5

Dewey Classification 793.8'5

A CIP record for this book is available
from the British Library

Photo acknowledgements
page 2 iStockphoto/Thinkstock;
4 Hemera/Thinkstock,
5 eAlisa/Shutterstock
Front cover Getty Images/
Thinkstock, iStockphoto/Thinkstock

Printed in China

Franklin Watts is a division of
Hachette Children's Books,
an Hachette company.
www.hachette.co.uk

EASY CARD TRICKS

Stephanie Turnbull

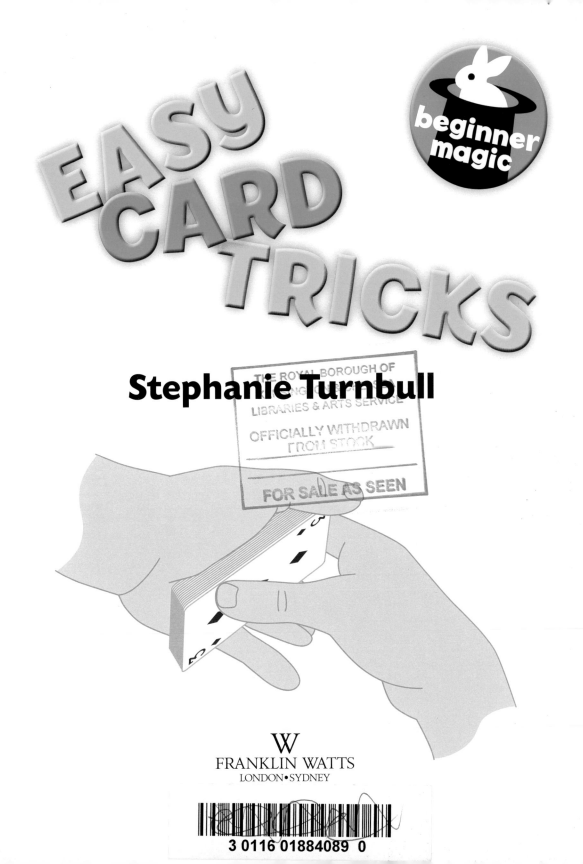

W
FRANKLIN WATTS
LONDON·SYDNEY

Note to Parents and Teachers

The READING ABOUT: STARTERS series introduces key science vocabulary to young children while encouraging them to discover and understand the world around them. The series works as a set of graded readers in three levels.

LEVEL 2: BEGIN TO READ ALONE follows guidelines set out in the National Curriculum for Year 2 in schools. These books can be read alone or as part of guided or group reading. Each book has three sections:

• Information pages that introduce key words. These key words appear in bold for easy recognition on pages where the related science concepts are explained.
• A lively story that recalls this vocabulary and encourages children to use these words when they talk and write.
• A quiz and index ask children to look back and recall what they have read.

Questions for Further Investigation

WHAT'S IN MY GARDEN explains key concepts about LOCAL WILDLIFE. Here are some suggestions for further discussion linked to questions on the information spreads:

p. 5 *Why do animals who live in your home hide away?* e.g. for safety. Ask children about size and type of animals that live in home. Also talk about nocturnal animals in the home.

p. 7 *Why do we need to put food out for birds in winter?* Explain that plants rest during the cold winter months as there is less sunshine to help them grow. As a result, there is less food such as nuts and berries. Also, there are less prey around, such as insects.

p. 11 *Why should you wash your hands after you touch soil?* Ask children about various safety issues when in garden, e.g. hygiene, water (ponds), stinging/biting animals.

p. 13 *Why do you think gardeners like to use compost?* Explain how rotting elements in soil help to feed growing flowers and vegetables with minerals and nutrients.

p. 15 *Why should you be still and quiet while watching animals?* e.g. so as not to scare them. Explain how many animals' only defence from hunters is to run or fly away.

p. 17 *What other sounds tell you that animals are near?* Ask children to divide sounds into groups, e.g. movement: rustling, splashing and calls: birdsong, squeaking, croaking.

p. 19 *Why do you think a spider hides near its web?* e.g. to ambush its prey. Could extend by asking children about why and how other animals hide, e.g. attack and defence.

p. 23 *What other nocturnal animals do you know?* e.g. cats, badgers, mice, bats, crickets. Ask children to think about how we know, e.g. sounds, trails, nibbled leaves, droppings.

ADVISORY TEAM

Educational Consultant
Andrea Bright – Science Co-ordinator, Trafalgar Junior School, Twickenham

Literacy Consultant
Jackie Holderness – former Senior Lecturer in Primary Education, Westminster Institute, Oxford Brookes University

Series Consultants
Anne Fussell – Early Years Teacher and University Tutor, Westminster Institute, Oxford Brookes University

David Fussell – C.Chem., FRSC

D0190882

CONTENTS

PAPERBACK EDITION PRINTED 2007
© Aladdin Books Ltd 2005

Designed and produced by
Aladdin Books Ltd
2/3 Fitzroy Mews
London W1T 6DF

First published in 2005
in Great Britain by
Franklin Watts
338 Euston Road
London NW1 3BH

Franklin Watts Australia
Hachette Children's Books
Level 17/207 Kent Street
Sydney NSW 2000

A catalogue record for this
book is available from the
British Library.
Dewey Classification: 577.5' 54
ISBN 978 07496 7524 0

Printed in Malaysia

All rights reserved

Editor: Jim Pipe

Design: Flick, Book Design
and Graphics

Thanks to: The pupils of Trafalgar
Infants School, Twickenham • Chloé,
Clara and Jean-Francois Guerif • The
pupils and teachers of Trafalgar Junior
School, Twickenham and St. Nicholas
C.E. Infant School, Wallingford.

Photocredits:
l-left, r-right, b-bottom, t-top,
c-centre, m-middle
Cover tl, tc & tr, 6, 8bl, 9tl, 10r, 12tr,
17 both, 20ml, 21br, 29tl, 29b, 31tr,
31br — Flick Smith. Cover b, 8t, 14tl,
20mr, 22tr, 23mr, 24ml, 25tr, 26mr,
27mr, 27b, 28tr, 30tr, 31bc — Jim
Pipe. 2tl, 9b, 11mr, 13t, 16, 18mr,
19mr, 28ml, 31tl — Otto Rogge
Photography. 2ml, 7tr, 14b, 18b, 23t,
26bl — US Fish & Wildlife Service.
2bl, 15 both, 31ml — Scott Bauer
/USDA. 3 — Comstock. 4, 10m —
Ken Hammond/USDA. 5tr, 31bl —
Select Pictures. 5b — John Foxx
Images. 7b, 13br, 25b, 29mr —
Stockbyte. 11t, 27tr both, 32 —
Ingram Publishing. 12b — USDA.
19t, 20b, 21t — Corel. 22b —
Corbis. 24br — Photodisc.

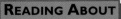

Starters

LOCAL WILDLIFE

What's in My Garden?

By Sally Hewitt

Aladdin/Watts
London • Sydney

Your **home** is the place where you live.
Your **home** is a **home** for
other animals, too.

You can find all kinds of animals
living all around you, if you know
where to look!

Garden

Animals live everywhere in the yard or **garden**, from the top of a tree to the bottom of a pond.

They also live inside your **home**, hiding in corners and under the floor.

Mice and other small animals make a home in walls.

• Why do animals who live in your home hide away?

Many **birds** perch in **trees** at night
and fly around in the daytime.
They visit gardens looking for food.

You can help **birds** in winter by leaving
out food and water for them to drink.

In spring, **birds** need somewhere safe to lay their eggs. They build **nests** in hidden places in bushes and **trees**.

If you see a **nest**, don't disturb it. A **nest** is a home for baby **birds**.

Nest

A bird box makes a safe home for a bird's nest.

• Why do we need to put food out for birds in winter?

Slugs and **snails** hide in **damp**, shady places. They come out at night and in the rain because they dry out in the sun.

Slug

Slugs and **snails** munch leaves.

You can see the holes they leave behind!

8

Slugs and **snails** have long, soft bodies. They make a slimy **trail** to help them slither along.

A **snail** has a curly shell on its back. It hides inside its shell to escape from danger.

Snail

• How are slugs and snails different?

Grass, flowers, and all kinds of
plants grow in **soil**.
Soil is home to many animals, too.

**Worms
in soil**

Worms live in **soil**. They eat **soil**
as they tunnel along underground.

This makes good **soil** for gardening.

10

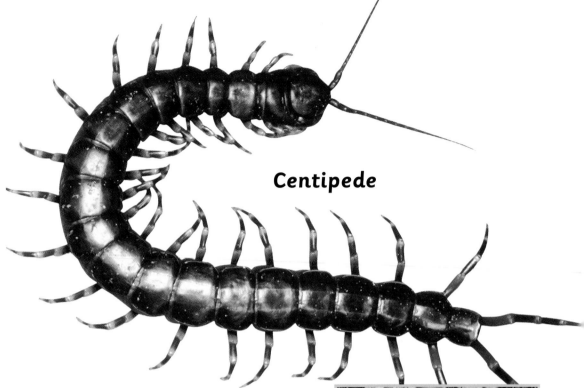

Centipede

Centipedes live in **soil** and lay their eggs there.

A **centipede** has many pairs of legs and can run very fast.

Centipedes hunt small animals for food.

Many small animals, such as ants, lay their eggs in soil.

• Why should you wash your hands after you touch soil?

Gardeners pile up cut grass and dead leaves to make a **compost** heap.

When the dead plants **rot,** they can be dug into soil to help plants grow.

Moss and fungi grow on logs to help them rot.

Woodlice

Animals that live in **compost** heaps help them to **rot**. Woodlice eat dead wood and plants.

Beetle

Some **beetles** lay their eggs in logs. The eggs hatch into larvae. The larvae eat wood and help it to **rot**.

• Why do you think gardeners like to use compost?

13

Many animals that fly visit **bushes** looking for food.

In the summer, **butterflies** sip sweet juice called nectar from flowers.

Caterpillars grow into butterflies. They munch leaves all day!

Butterfly

Tiny insects called **aphids** cling to stems and leaves. They suck out juice called sap. This can damage plants.

Aphid

Ladybugs fly onto hedges and **bushes** looking for **aphids** to eat.

Ladybug

• Why should you be still and quiet while you are watching animals?

Bee

Many **flowers** have bright colors and sweet smells.

Bees see the colors, smell the smells, and land on the **flowers** to sip sugary nectar.

16

You can hear **bees, wasps,** and **flies** buzz when they fly. Buzzing is the sound of their wings moving.

Wasps and **flies** like to eat ripe fruit. They feed on fruit that has fallen on the ground.

Bees help plants by carrying pollen from flower to flower.

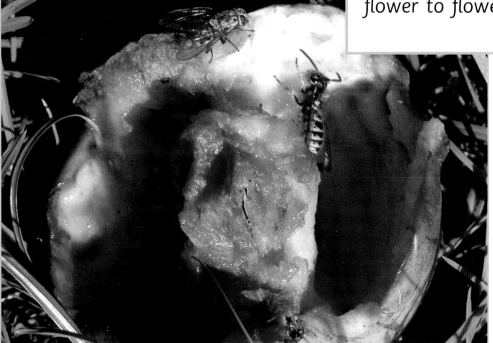

• What other sounds tell you that animals are near?

Spiders spin **webs** between stalks of grass, in branches, and in corners of rooms.

A **spider's web** is like a net for catching food.

Spider

An insect flies into a **web**. The **spider** runs out and wraps it in silk to eat later.

Ants

Ants follow each other in trails across **grass** and paths.

They find food and carry it back to their nest in the soil.

An ants' nest is full of tunnels and rooms where the ants lay their eggs.

• Why do you think a spider hides near its web?

A **pond** makes a good home for many different animals.

Goldfish dart about under the water.

If you visit a pond, always take an adult with you.

Frogs, toads, and **newts** swim in the water and hide in damp grass around the **pond**.

Newt

20

Diving beetle

Diving beetles and other small animals hunt under the water.

Pond skaters skim across the surface of the water.

Colorful **dragonflies** hang on the stalks of plants that grow on the bank.

Dragonfly

• Why might hungry animals visit a pond?

Hedgehog

Nocturnal animals come out in the garden to **hunt** at night.

A hedgehog **hunts** for worms and small animals.

An owl swoops out of the sky to **hunt** mice with its sharp claws.

Owl

Raccoon

Nocturnal animals may leave signs behind them.

Foxes and raccoons **hunt** for food in trash cans.

Footprints tell you who has been in your yard.

• What other nocturnal animals do you know?

TARA AND TESS GO WILD!

Look out for words about **local wildlife.**

Tess and Tara ran out of their new **home** into the **garden**.

"Look!" said Tess. "The **garden** is like a jungle!"

"Let's explore," said Tess. She jumped into the long **grass**.

"Stop!" said Tara. "Why?" asked Tess. Then she saw it—a big **spider** sitting in its **web**.

24

"Don't break the **web**!" said Tara.
Suddenly, something flew up out
of the **grass**. They jumped.

"What's that?" asked Tara.
"It's only a **bird**," said Tess.
It might have a **nest** in that **tree**!"
said Tara. "There's a **worm** in its beak."

"Where did the **worm** come from?"
asked Tess.

25

"**Worms** live in the **soil**," said Tara. She bent down. "There are so many **flowers** and weeds I can't see any **soil**!"

"I can," said Tess. "Look, there are **footprints** in the **soil**."

Dad came into the **garden** carrying his **garden** tools.

"**Nocturnal hunters** like foxes probably made those **footprints**," said Dad.

"Come on. There's lots of **gardening** to do!"

"Stop!" said Tess and Tara.

"The **garden** is full of animals."

"We can share it with them," said Dad.

It was hot the next day. **Flies** and **wasps** buzzed about in the air. Dad mowed the **grass**. Tara pulled up weeds and found an **ants' nest**.

Tess explored and found an empty **pond**.

"Can you help me move this log?" asked Dad. "It's full of **woodlice** and **beetles**!" said Tara. "They make the log **rot** away," said Dad.

"Look! A **centipede**," said Tess. "All its legs tickled my hand!"

Tess showed Dad and Tara the empty **pond**. It was full of **slugs** and **snails** and their silver **trails**.

"**Slugs** and **snails** like **damp** places," said Dad.

"Can we fill the **pond** with water?" asked Tess. "I love **frogs!**"
"Ooh yes! And can we plant **flowers** for the **bees** and **butterflies**?" asked Tara.

"Yes. And we'll plant honeysuckle **bushes** for moths to visit at night," said Dad.

"I'll make a **bird** table for the **birds** too," said Dad. "You two can help me."

"Animals will be wild about our **garden**," said Tara.

Dad laughed. "And we'll love living in our new **home,** too," he said.

Make a list of the animals you have seen in your **garden** or your favorite park. Draw pictures to show where they live.

A wriggly worm lives in the soil.

This bird's nest is in a tree.

QUIZ

Why don't **slugs** and **snails**
come out in the sun?

Answer on page 8

How do animals like **woodlice**
help a **compost** heap?

Answer on pages 12-13

How might **ladybugs**
help gardeners?

Answer on page 15

What animals would you find living
in these parts of a garden or home?

Inside

Pond

Soil

Have you read this book? Well done! Do you remember these words? Look back and find out.

INDEX